THAT SATURDAY NIGHT

Sally Crooks

for Ed,
with best wishes and
happy memories of S.W.
and Fort San.
Sally

TRAFFORD
PUBLISHING

Cover art by Antoinette Hérivel

Note for Librarians: A cataloguing record for this book is available from Library and Archives Canada at www.collectionscanada.ca/amicus/index-e.html
ISBN 1-4120-6965-3

Printed in Victoria, BC, Canada. Printed on paper with minimum 30% recycled fibre. Trafford's print shop runs on "green energy" from solar, wind and other environmentally-friendly power sources.

Offices in Canada, USA, Ireland and UK
This book was published *on-demand* in cooperation with Trafford Publishing. On-demand publishing is a unique process and service of making a book available for retail sale to the public taking advantage of on-demand manufacturing and Internet marketing. On-demand publishing includes promotions, retail sales, manufacturing, order fulfilment, accounting and collecting royalties on behalf of the author.

Book sales for North America and international:
Trafford Publishing, 6E–2333 Government St.,
Victoria, BC V8T 4P4 CANADA
phone 250 383 6864 (toll-free 1 888 232 4444)
fax 250 383 6804; email to orders@trafford.com
Book sales in Europe:
Trafford Publishing (UK) Limited, 9 Park End Street, 2nd Floor
Oxford, UK OX1 1HH UNITED KINGDOM
phone 44 (0)1865 722 113 (local rate 0845 230 9601)
facsimile 44 (0)1865 722 868; info.uk@trafford.com
Order online at:
trafford.com/05-1876

10 9 8 7 6 5 4

for my family,
and in memory of my husband Jim,
and all my Anderson family

Acknowledgments

The following prose pieces first appeared in *Lodestone: Stories by Regina Writers*, **Fifth House Publishers** (1993): *Journey, The Greenock House, Uncle Hammy's Flat, The Shop, On a Summer Morning, On the Sea, Adam,* and *Dream Ship.*

Her Mother was first published in CVII, Fall, 1989.

I would like to thank the following people whose interest and encouragement over the years have helped me tell this story: Fred Wah, Paulette Jiles, Ven Begamudre, Allan Safarik, Dave Margoshes, Susan Crean and Joanne Gerber.

Thank you also to Antoinette Hérivel for the cover art and the photograph, A Prairie Sea.

Contents

1. *Above:* A Prairie Sea, Saskatchewan, 2005

2. *Left:* Catriona and Andrew take a last look at Scotland from the *Empress of Canada*, July 6, 1965.

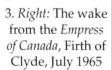

3. *Right:* The wake from the *Empress of Canada*, Firth of Clyde, July 1965

Prologue:

Journey 1965

When I left for a new life across the seas with my husband and two small children, we sailed up overnight from Liverpool, in the *Empress of Canada*, and awoke in the early morning at the "Tail o' the Bank" the furthermost reaches of the River Clyde. The ship lay off-shore at Greenock and waited for its Scottish passengers. Most people on board watched the tender as it left the pier, but I was looking beyond the pier and beyond the railway station to the house in Brougham Street where I had spent my childhood summers. With the binoculars I found the attic window, focused, and brought the image up sharp and clear. In the early morning sun its three angled panes reflected glints of gold in the grey slate roof.

Then I heard the bagpipe music, faint at first but gradually louder as the small boat drew near. A disembodied sound, it reached the ear, an echo from distant battles and long-dead chiefs and princes: *Up the Blue Bonnets, The Dark Island, Will Ye No' Come Back Again?*. Sounding over the water, it might have been for an ancient king, borne on dream-green Hebridean seas to the holy Isle of Iona, there to be carried along the Street of the Dead and laid with old saints in the sacred earth.

I was sailing in a luxury liner. It took five days to cross the Atlantic Ocean. Every day I would stand in the stern and watch the sea churn and swirl up from the propellers. The wake streamed behind, at first creamy-white and green, like the marble of Iona, then jet-black and smooth. This street of black and white and green stretched back,

1

back to the islands the ship had left, the Street of the Dead along which seamen had been brought in convoy to remain forever, the sudden white flash of explosion in their eyes. Following the way of seamen and kings, I journeyed also towards an undiscovered country, but travelled backwards, facing east, looking back to Scotland and the attic above the grey house. I saw a figure at the window. It was a ten-year-old girl.

I
GREENOCK
1930's

The Greenock House

The first Andersons in my family came from the Highlands at the time of the Clearances, a time when landlords decided sheep were a more valuable commodity than people. They at least found work in the new railway industry in the west of Scotland. Many others were forced to emigrate. By the 1930's the house in which my Greenock relatives lived was already old: a soot-grimed tenement building of grey sandstone beside the railway. There were uncles, aunts and cousins on all three storeys. Aunt Sarah, my father's sister, lived with her family on the third floor in a large flat with an attic above. The trains crossed the railway bridge over Brougham Street past the side window of the parlour. From there I used to wave to the engine drivers. One of them might be Uncle Hammy. His name was Hamilton, but everyone called him Hammy.

Whenever I smell lavender, I am transported to Aunt Sarah's parlour, sitting on the green velvet, antimacassared couch, the material tickling the backs of my bare legs, white-sandaled feet scarcely reaching the faded carpet. Hearing the chuffing of a steam engine, I rush to the window. It might be my uncle watching for me and ready to return my excited wave. He seems so close I could almost touch his outstretched hand. I always see him like this, framed in the iron window opening of the locomotive: blue dungarees, red bandana at his neck, peaked railwayman's cap set at a rakish angle, white teeth flashing a smile on his grimy face.

From the attic window, with my cousin Andrew's telescope, I scan the Firth of Clyde for ships, mostly small merchant vessels delivering their cargoes of coal or manufactured goods to the Western Isles, or pleasure steamers taking their cargoes of holiday-makers "doon the watter" to the pretty seaside towns of Gourock, Dunoon or Rothesay. The ocean-going liners, headed for America or Canada, sometimes lie off-shore waiting to pick up their Scottish passengers, and I never tire of gazing at them through the telescope; never tire of imagining the life of glamour and adventure to which they are sailing

Uncle Hammy's Flat

Uncle Hammy is my father's older brother. He lives in a second floor flat immediately below Aunt Sarah's. It is noisy and crowded with seven sons and a daughter. It fascinates me that houses identical in layout can feel so different because of the people who live there. When I'm tired of the company in one, I move either up or down to the other and feel equally at home.

At Uncle Hammy's I remember Sunday afternoon card games around the kitchen table, and my cousins cranking up the gramophone and pushing aside the furniture to practise the latest dance steps: *Jealousy* for the tango, and *South of the Border* for the slow foxtrot. Their mother ineffectually threatens the wrath of God on her brood of sinning sons, who so blatantly neglect to keep the Sabbath day holy.

On Saturday nights the boys brush their brilliantined hair, give their shoes a last minute shine with *Cherry Blossom Boot Polish*, and flick a speck of fluff from their Oxford "bags" before dashing off to take the current girlfriend to picture house or dance hall. Adam is my favourite among Uncle Hammy's boys, perhaps because we share the same name. We both have been given Aunt Sarah's name. He has her married surname, and I have both that and her Christian name, after the Scottish custom. I am happily spoilt by all these grown-up relatives, especially Adam. He once took me to the summer show at Gourock and bought me a box of chocolates as though I were already grown up and his girlfriend, or as though he were my father home on shore leave taking me out for a special treat, and I was just myself.

Memory Is a Fragrance

On my Greenock holidays I stay at Aunt Sarah's. She has only slightly more room for me than Uncle Hammy. My cousins, Jess and Myra, and my Aunt Mary have their bedrooms in the attic. I have to sleep with one of them. My choice is always with the slim and beautiful Jess, my dream in reality of what I hope to look like in another ten or so years. But when she's had enough of this wriggling, fidgety thing in her bed, I am passed to poor asthmatic Myra or, worse still, to Aunt Mary, who snores.

Memory is a fragrance. The bedrooms are *Coty* face powder, *Evening in Paris* perfume, *Sloan's Liniment* and peppermint.

The rooms on the main floor fan out from a wide circular hall. Uncle Robert, Aunt Sarah's second husband and step-father to my cousins, is secretary of the Railwaymen's Union, and his office, to which men come on railway business, is a little room just inside the front door. Uncle Robert is a mild-mannered, elderly gentleman with a soft Aberdeenshire accent, who lets me play by the hour with his typewriter, rubber stamps, paperclips and carbon paper. Even today the smells of paper and ink and pencils can take me back to that tiny room.

But the serious business of the day is conducted in the kitchen, every morning after breakfast, in a haze of cigarette smoke. "What will I wear today, Mother?" asks Cousin Jess, elegant in the black silk kimono brought from Japan by her merchant seaman fiance.

This is my father's home too, but never when I am here. I search for him, for traces of his presence. Perhaps

he's here in the man-smells of pipe tobacco, shaving soap,
brilliantine on brushes.

On a Summer Morning

Aunt Sarah and I wait in Brougham Street for the bus. It will stop right opposite our house. I hop up and down, part impatience, part excitement, and partly to keep warm in my cotton print dress and cardigan, for the early morning air is chilly. How fresh and clean the air is with the wind coming off the Firth of Clyde carrying sea scent! The sky is a faded blue, not bright, gently merging with pink-tinged clouds – like tie-dye. And always the sound of sea gulls as they soar and dip, foraging for breakfast. You might hear the sonorous base of a liner's horn out on the firth and the answering tenor and alto of merchant-men or tugs. The streets have a clean, washed look after an overnight shower. The senses mingle. The tang of sea is the cry of gulls. The stroke of breeze, the pale tint of sky.

Aunt Sarah holds me by the hand and laughs at my hopping antics, letting her hand jerk up and down with mine. She always wears gloves in the street, winter and summer, so her grasp is the smooth softness of kid or cotton encasing her plump hand. She is always soft – her round body in winter fur or summer silk, her petal skin, and her white hair waving around her head to the bun just above the nape of her neck. Her hats are rich velour, mulberry or black, or cool raffia straw the colour of sand. They have veils. In winter they fit under the chin with elastic; in summer they cover only half her face. I see her smile, but her eyes are hidden. She veils the winters of her life – a sickly child, a husband's death, a brother's erring ways. Over her voice with the lilt of sea waves is the counterpoint of laughter, the constant inshore ripples. You scarcely hear the ground bass in the music of her life or hear the ground swell of its ocean.

Where I live now in Saskatchewan, a sea of green prairie laps the city's shorelines, and the ocean breaks open its box of fragrant spikenard two thousand miles to the east and a thousand miles to the west. The stare of blue sky is intense, the push of hot wind insistent, and on the elm's dead branch raucous crows argue over breakfast. From where I stand outside my house, waiting for the downtown bus, I can hear the snarling roar of a jet revving up for take-off. It lifts from its dusty lair and mounts up and up and over my head into the bleached and parched morning air. The sound and fury of its fiery breath diminish as it fades into the eastern sky where still there lingers a blue-pink haze.

But it is the same sky that, wrapped in a grey shroud, swept down on endless Atlantic waves, or mingled, unobtrusive, among blue-green Hebridean Isles. It is the same sky that, while I slept and dreamt, was seen, perhaps, by some small girl five thousand miles away. Did she see it through a soft sea haze as she watched the darting gulls, or marvel at its limitless blue framed in an attic skylight window?

The Shop

The delicious aroma of a box of chocolate bars freshly opened; the pungent smells of newsprint and tobacco; the rough, kindly accents of the Clydeside working folk as they ask for their sweeties or their newspapers, for an ounce of *Saint Bruno Flake* tobacco or a packet of *Woodbine* cigarettes. It is Aunt Sarah's shop, in the east end of Greenock, among the engineering works and shipyards along the banks of the Firth of Clyde. The shop has to open very early in the morning to sell newspapers to the workers, and for the boys to pick up their loads for delivery. All day long there is a continual flow of customers. Housewives, out shopping for the day's bread and butchermeat, call for their weekly magazine. There are few, coming in with their children, who escape without being coaxed to hand over pennies for candy or a comic – or even a toy. Then, at the end of the day, in troop the men again for their *Evening News* or *Citizen*.

A day at the shop lasts from early morning to early evening, and so we eat our meals right there in the back shop. Like the housewives, we go shopping for the day's provisions: meat from the butcher for mid-day dinner, fish from the fish-monger for high tea or, maybe from the baker – along with the bread, tea-bread and cream-cake treats – the favourite mutton pies. The men from the ships, when asked on their first day home, "And what would you like for your tea?" might answer, "Just a pie, thanks. And oh, er… maybe a cream cookie?"

Although the days at the shop are long, I'm never bored. How could I be, with comics to read and toys to play with, especially the dolls that cry "Mama" and close their eyes when you lay them down? If I get tired of playing in the back shop, I hang around behind the counter. It's then I'm tempted to spend some of my holiday pocket money on sweets (I'm not indulged to the extent of free candy) from the enormous assortment in the shop There are boxes of chocolates at which children and those who have to count their bawbees can only gaze. On a Saturday, a young fellow might buy a box for his girlfriend – Cadbury's *Roses*, Rowntree's *Black Magic* or Terry's *All Gold*. The other chocolate box buyers are usually men on shore leave. They come in for their papers and cigarettes and, in a mood of indulgence, buy chocolates for the wife who sits lonely hours by the fire and turns the heel of the navy blue sock on its slender needles, or for the child who sits at the end of the kitchen table and draws pictures of ships billowing black smoke against gun-metal sea and sky.

Some of these men know my father. When they ask my aunt, "Well, an' who's this bonnie lassie?" she answers, "Oh, this is Tommy's wee girlie." Tommy's wee girlie. I like that. Although I have never seen him, these words make me feel I belong to both. To Aunt Sarah he is a brother, like my brother Tom to me. To these men he is Tommy, a man they know, perhaps have sweated alongside in the thirsty, throbbing depths of a ship's engine room, or chatted with over a pint in the pub. I imagine him, like them, in his straight, merchant seaman's navy blue coat and peaked cap.

I think...what if one day the shop door suddenly jangles open and he bursts in straight off the ship? Will my aunt say, "This is your wee girlie, Tommy."? And will we then, after our back shop tea of pies and cream cookies, catch the bus back home to Brougham Street? If we do, my father – my daddy – will have to help me up the stairs to the top of the bus where I like to ride, for I will be carrying a new doll – the one with long fringed lashes on eyes that close – and the biggest box of *All Gold* you can possibly buy in any shop.

II
KILMARNOCK
1940's

The Kilmarnock House

The house in which I lived in Kilmarnock with my mother and two older sisters was, like the Greenock house, built of grey sandstone – austere, forbidding. Inside, the hallway, a place of shadows in our blacked-out, war-time world, narrowed to the cavern depths of back porch, wash house, coal cellar. This was the panic place, the thumping heart louder than the clang of shovel and pail. The darkness, blacker than the glinting coal, stopped the voice in its fearful prayers, incantations against the nameless horrors of the imagination. And the stairway, echoing stone and steep, led to the landing, where, on the window seat, the paraffin lamp, its tongue of flame flickering from the upturned mouth of ruby glass, beaconed the way upstairs. It was not always dark in this remembered house, but when a chink between curtains could mean a German bomb (or so they said) and the door to the street had to open from darkness to darkness, dark is what I recall.

But this house, just like the Greenock house, also had an attic. I loved to play there. I would climb the wooden spiral, hands groping for the banister, eyes looking up to the rectangle of blue or grey or tattered white, framed in the skylight window on the landing. How strange to look through a window and see only the limitless sky! The doors from the landing led to a large bedroom, the box room with its unused steamer trunk and junk-filled boxes, and to the loft, the exposed pipes and rafters under the gabled, slated roof. It was here that the iron pipes would freeze in winter and burst with the expanding ice. The water, as the ice thawed, would seep through the ceiling to the rooms below.

The attic was the place of adventure, of limitless possibility in games of make-believe. The doors became entrances to secret rooms in fairy-tale castles, to ballrooms in Hollywood mansions, and to staterooms in ocean liners. I would dress up in my sisters' clothes hanging in the large wardrobe or drape myself in the ever-present remnants and lengths of material my mother kept there until she found time to make them up for us.

When I was older I would take my school books up to the attic to do my homework but find myself drawn to the bedroom window, a three-directional Cyclops eye from which I watched the flotsam and jetsam of a wartime industrial town: blue-overalled factory workers, the women's hair tucked into scarf turbans; gas-masked, white-tin-hatted air-raid wardens; and kit-bagged, black bereted soldiers going to North Africa or returning from Italy, all, so it seemed to me, swept along the dreary, grey street on an endless and relentless current of war effort.

When we moved from that house, I was sorry to leave the attic, but I took it with me in my mind. I would have liked to leave behind the dark downstairs, but it insisted on coming too.

The Coal Cellar

Our coal cellar is a lean-to behind the house. I unlock the door. Coal is scarce; someone might steal it. I have to stoop a little as though entering a cave. No one ever remembers to get the coal in the daylight; now I have to get it. I have brought the Ever-ready flashlight, but it doesn't help. I am afraid of the dark. *God is our refuge and our strength/ In straits a present aid/ Therefore although the earth remove/ We will not be afraid.* No time to sing it like the Covenanters – those defenders of religious freedom in old Scotland – bravely and defiantly, whether the king's men came or not – no Anglican Church for them. I say it as quickly as I can, time after time, to make the magic stronger, but that doesn't help either. I am still afraid. I pile the pieces of coal in the pail, large ones first, then smaller and smallest, building the fire in reverse. The other pail is the dross pail. I shovel in the dross for banking the fire at night. The embers underneath will still be glowing bright red in the morning. I clang the shovel and pail as loudly as I can, but that doesn't help either. I think of ships where engines clang and clatter from port to distant port. There too the fires will never go out. The stokers shovel in caverns of coal in the ship's bunker, an undersea mine. My sister Margaret has coal gloves, but my hands are black – perhaps like my father's – black with the dust from fossil forests where aeons ago man stooped as he walked, wary-eyed, fearing the unknown and talking to his gods.

Family Matters

I never heard my mother sing the song Margaret kept talking and talking about all these years. It was an Irish song called *Kathleen Mavourneen*. I think mavourneen means "my little one". Anyway, what Margaret said was that our dad would listen to Mum singing this song in her beautiful voice, and then he would play the tune on the cornet. She told me that one summer at the band camp, he went up into the woods by himself to practise, and he played *Kathleen Mavourneen*. When he got back, the men said to him, "God, Tommy, how did you learn to play like that?" "By listening to my wife singing," he said.

I remember once someone sang this song on TV. I watched Margaret as she listened. She was forming the words along with the singer, and crying. She was eleven when our mother left him.

Jennie was fourteen. She left school to work in the warehouse of a shoe factory, bobbed her long hair, so Margaret said, and set her mouth in a thin, straight line. Her eyes (they were grey-green like all the Andersons') were often sad, even angry and sulky, but not when she rode Grandpa McKinnon's black hunter. She sailed over the jumps and brought him red first-place tickets for the tack room walls. She was Grandpa's favourite. In her riding boots and breeches she looked like the picture of his tall, fair son, the one who didn't come back from South Africa.

On cold winter nights, going home from Grandma's, she would race me between the lamp posts so it wouldn't seem so far. She taught me to ride and to set my mouth in a thin line when things got bad. On Saturday afternoons she waited for me at my dancing class. I didn't know anyone else whose sister took her to see the ballet whenever it came to Glasgow.

My brother Tom was only five when the break up came. Old enough to remember; too young to understand. When I was five he took me to kindergarten – the first day – then abandoned me. He was a harum-scarum, always in trouble, but laughing, an infectious, gutsy giggle. After the Saturday matinee, he would posture in front of the mirror. "Stick em' up!" he'd say to Jimmy Cagney. He loved to whistle, and he tap-danced up and down the stone stairs à la Fred Astaire. We had to laugh, even Jennie.

I remember one Christmas when I was still expecting Santa, Tom found where the toys were hidden. When Mum was out he produced them before my astonished eyes. His toy was a small but heavy red-painted tractor with rubber treads. Its weight and traction let it climb over obstacles in its path – even feet. I said it was a tractor, but he insisted it was a tank.

Tom and I played guessing games with up-turned plates and knives, tapping and rattling the rhythms of songs we knew till one or the other guessed or gave up. Margaret would listen and say, "You get your rhythm from Daddy, you two," and then add, "He was a lovely dancer."

When I was ten Tom ran away.

Saturday Night Chore

Half past six on a Saturday night, Margaret and I do dishes. She washes; I dry. Scottish dance music reels and jigs from the old Marconi on the broad window shelf. Fiddles, accordions, vamping piano send urgent messages to restless toes. Familiar tunes – *Drops o' Brandy, Kate Dalrymple, De'il amang the Tailors* – take command of feet and voices. We la-la and hum, half-dance on the spot.

Margaret washes plates; I dry cups and saucers. Free of the sink, I extend my dancing space, venture *pas-de-bas*, skip-change-of-step to the table and back while drying plates. A voice announces, "A Scottish Waltz Medley". Margaret resists no longer. Without a word, as if on cue, in one continuous, rapid movement, she grabs the dish towel, dries hands, kicks off shoes, and waltzes me round the kitchen.

She sings (a little off key) each successive old favourite – *Oh, ye'll tak the high road an' I'll tak the low road, an' I'll be in Scotland afore ye…..Speed, bonnie boat like a bird on the wing, 'Onward' the sailors cry…..Come o'er the stream, Chairlie, dear Chairlie, fine Chairlie, Come o'er the stream, Chairlie, an' dine wi' Maclean.* Birling, swinging round table and chairs, we giggle and clown, sing with mock passion, *When you and I were young, Maggie, when you and I…were…..young.*

The Dick Institute

When I send my annual subscription to the Burns Federation, an international association for promotion of the works of the poet, Robert Burns, I mail it to Dean Castle, Kilmarnock, for that is where the headquarters of the Federation is located, but for many years, the Dick Institute, Kilmarnock was an address familiar to Burnsians the world over as the Federation's home. In continuing my membership in this organization, I'm maintaining an annual link with two places important in my early life. The grounds of Dean Castle, which dates from medieval times, were a favourite place for Sunday afternoon rambles. The Dick Institute was almost as much a part of my childhood and youth as were the schools I attended.

"The Dick" is museum, library, art gallery and lecture hall. There, the world of books opened up for me with my first library card. My schoolgirl friend Ray and I made regular Saturday visits, progressing from junior library favorites like *Anne of Green Gables* whose island home we discovered at the eastern edge of a huge land mass coloured in pink on the wall map, to the more sophisticated offerings of the senior library.

During the war the lecture hall was used to show Ministry of Information films with titles like *Our Backs to the Land*, or *Our Ships at Sea.* The attraction of these films was, for us, purely social in that they provided, in an evening and with parental approval, a place to go that was free, dry, and relatively warm. The theme music for the series, I later discovered, was not, as one might have expected, some patriotic, soul-stirring melody by

Elgar or Vaughan-Williams, but the *Moldau* section of another great patriotic work, *Ma Vlast* (My Country) by the Czech composer, Smetana. The sound depiction of the Vltava River, surging and soaring with ever-increasing volume and intensity, is forever linked in my mind with the steamy smells of damp gabardine, wool berets and school caps, and adolescent feet in rubber "Wellies"; with whispers and giggles shushed by the irascible janitor; and with black and white images of windy landscapes, sturdy Land Army girls toiling for absent farmers, and corvettes and merchantmen dipping, rising and dipping again through towering Atlantic waves.

In 1950, Ray and I, each embarking on a career in music, she as a pianist, I as a singer, gave a song recital in the art gallery/lecture hall. In our desire to impress, we performed *Arie Antiche* – early Italian songs – German *Lieder*, French *Chansons* and English Art Songs, but not one song by Robert Burns – who had indisputable ties to the building in which we were performing.

In recent times, the Dick Institute has also become a centre for genealogical research, and on my last visit there, in 1998, Ray accompanied me as I peered into the past, scanning the microfiches for my Anderson ancestors. On that visit, too, we talked about how our lives had unfolded, hers in Scotland, mine in Canada, and how we had been linked in lifelong friendship, not only by our background and shared interests, but also by the single most traumatic event of my childhood that happened one Saturday night.

4. Self aged 4 with Greenock
cousins

5. Self in the backyard beside
railway

6. *Above:* Aunt Mary L. and Aunt
Sarah, 1920's

7. *Right:* Mother, L. and Aunt
Sarah, 1930's

26

8. *Left*: Sister Jennie L. and cousin Jess, Greenock esplanade, 1930's

9. *Right*: Self and Margaret in Aunt Sarah's parlour, 1940's

10. *Left*: Self, mother and sisters, 1938

27

III
STORIES

My Father's Story 1942

1. *On the Sea*

Where did ye say ye came frae, Alex? Ayr? Burns country, eh? That's no' far frae Kilmarnock. Ma wife's frae Kilmarnock. What's yer poison? Whisky? Bob! Owre here, Bob! Ma pal here'll have a dram an' a chaser – aye, a half an' a half pint. I'll have the same. Now where was I? Oh, aye.

As I was tellin' ye, what I remember most is the *greyness* an' the red on Jimmie Patterson's chest. Everythin' else was swamped in this grey mist. We didnae know who else had got off the ship. Most o' them, we thought, might be in the lifeboats, but we couldnae see. I hated to think that some o' the lads might have been trapped below.

There was this fog, you see, an' there were four o' us on the raft, an' that was because we were the ones, along wi' the captain, who were last off. That's what happens. The engineers an' the stokers have got to stay there to keep the ship movin' – even zig-zaggin' about. As long as there's any hope o' gettin' away frae the U boats, you've got to stay there; you've got to stay there below till the captain says, "Abandon Ship."

Well, the raft, the Carley float they call it, was the only thing that was left for us – Jimmie, an' John Mackenzie an' Hughie Boyd an' me, Tom Anderson. But we couldnae see the captain.

It was a long day. We didnae see another soul, another ship, another lifeboat, but we hoped that when the fog began to lift, this wee raft, like a dinghy, away out in the middle o' the Atlantic would be seen, that an aeroplane or a ship would spot us. The plane, of course, could signal to a ship to pick us up.

I wasnae really very worried because I had been torpedoed before – several times. I was the "Chiefy", so I tried to keep these young fellows' spirits up by encouragin' them, tellin' them it wouldnae be long, that sooner or later somebody was bound to see us. But what did worry me was Jimmie Patterson lyin' there, that red stain gettin' bigger an' bigger across his chest, an' him coughin'.

The rest o' us were a' right, but we were soaked, soaked to the skin. Our clothes stuck to our bodies like another skin gradually growin' there, stiff an' hard, as the sea water dried. An' we were cold. We knew we needed the wind to clear away the fog. But the stronger the wind got, the colder we got. I just kept hopin' it would clear quick, that the sun would come through an' warm us up a wee bit. We had to slap at oursel'es an' wiggle our toes an' our fingers. We couldnae very well stamp our feet. We had to move as much as we could to keep the circulation goin'. But poor Jimmie. He had just to lie there. The only movement he got was his heavin' shoulders an' chest as he coughed.

Well, the long day dragged by. It was nearly night time before we saw, far away in the distance, one o' the escort ships that had been detailed to look for survivors. My, that was a sicht for sair een, I'm tellin' you. But when we got on board we knew that before very long three o' us would be back on the Atlantic run.

As for Jimmie – I wondered if I would be the one that would have to tell his wife.

2. Fiona

The captain said, "Would you like me to go, Chief?" An' I said, "No, sir. I've known Patterson all his life. I sailed wi' his father when I was young. I know Jimmie's wife too, Bill Campbell's daughter. A fine young lassie she is, wi' two wee bairns. It's the least I can do for Jimmie."

Fiona was livin' in Glasgow wi' her mother, an' I thought if I got there about dinner time she wouldnae be by herself. I got the 10 o'clock train from Greenock Central to Glasgow an' then the tram out to Brig'ton. I found the street an' the house – a nice wee bungalow – wi' nae bother.

I rang the doorbell an' waited, thinkin' I should have stopped at the pub on the way up to stiffen my back. Then the door opened, an' here was this wee bit lass wi' her red Campbell hair down to her shoulders, an' her baby in her arms an' wee Jamie hangin' on to her skirt. She didnae look old enough to be a wife let alone a mother. When I saw her my courage nearly left me altogether.

"Hullo, Fiona lass," I said. My voice sounded funny to me, kind o' high-pitched an' unnatural.

"Mr. Anderson!" she said. "Come away in." But even as she spoke, I could tell she knew there was somethin' wrong. She was lookin' at me wi' these big brown eyes o' hers as if she could read what was in my face. Wi' that her mother came out o' the kitchen dryin' her hands on her apron. "Oh, it's you, Tommy," she said. "This is a surprise." Then, "My God! What is it?"

"You'd better sit down," I said. "Come on, lass." I took Fiona's hand an' led her into the livin' room. Her mother made to take the baby, but Fiona held on to her as though she'd never let her go an' pulled Jamie close beside her.

Then I told them as gently as I could, an' gave Fiona Jimmie's things he'd had on him when we were hit. It wasnae much. His watch an' his weddin' ring an' a wee silver Iona cross Fiona had given him. We had left the letters an' photos in his wallet. They were too badly stained, so they went into the sea wi' Jimmie.

Seaman's Lullaby

Sh, bairnie, sh!
Dinna greet, ma dearie.
Come tae Dad, ma bonnie lamb,
Ah'll kiss awa' the tearie.

Your Daddy has a great big boat
for sailin' owre the sea.
An' if ye're good an' greet nae mair,
Ah'll tak ye there wi' me.
Sh, bairnie, sh!

3. That Saturday Night

After I had been to see Jimmie's wife, I went to a pub an' had a few, hopin' they would make me feel better, but they didnae. I kept thinkin' o' Fiona lookin' at me as if she couldnae take in what I was sayin', then gettin' up to take goodbye wi' me, an' standin' at the door still holdin' on to her bairns for dear life. An' the wee ones, growin' up without their dad. Then it hit me. They were the same age my two youngest had been the last time I saw them. I thought, my God, that poor soul has no man to look after her now – a wife without a husband. An' here am I, a husband wi' a wife that doesnae want him. Well, after I had sat there for a while thinkin' about it an' rememberin' I had nearly copped it too, I decided I would take the train down to Kilmarnock an' try an' see Jen. I thought, what the hell! She can tell me to my face she doesnae want any more to do wi' me. I had tried to see her before but never managed it, an' I had written to her off an' on for nearly fourteen years, but she never answered my letters. She wouldnae let me see the bairns either. Sarah told me young Tom had joined the army – the Royal Scots Greys – an' was in the Middle East. I heard the Greys were in Haifa when I was there wi' a tanker, but I'm damned if he wasnae away on some sortie, an' that was that.

Anyway, back to my story about goin' to Kilmarnock. I had another couple o' drams an' went to Saint Enoch's for the train. It was nearly dark by the time I got to Kilmarnock, but I knew the road a' right. I knew they were livin' in that big grey sandstone house in Old Mill Road, the one belongin' to her father. I suspected the old skinflint was makin' her pay rent, for Sarah – that's my sister – had told me there was another family rentin' the bottom flat.

Well, when I got there I rang the doorbell an' waited. There was a kind o' watery moon, an' that helped to make the blackout a bit less black. I was just lookin' up at the clouds an' wonderin' if I was goin' to get back to Glasgow that night before it rained, when I realized the door had opened. I couldnae see very well who was there because it was dark inside too, but I didnae think it was my wife. So I said, "Is Mrs. Anderson at home?" A voice just said, "No, she's not." It sounded like a young girl answerin', maybe one o' the family downstairs. I thought, God! I've come a' this way an' she's no' even here. "Do you know when she'll be back?" I asked. I thought maybe they were well enough acquainted that she'd know that, but she didnae. I just thanked her an' left. All I could think o' was – what a bloody waste o' time!

4. Struck Dumb

Do you mind I told you, Alex, how I went to Kilmarnock that Saturday night last November to try an' see my wife? Well, you'll never believe what I'm goin' to tell you. I got back to Glasgow in a mood as black as the Earl o' Hell's waistcoat. I just had time to doss down for a few hours at the Seamen's Union, an' then I had to be up at the crack o' dawn (sore head an' a') to catch my boat. I didnae even have time to look in home at Brougham Street to say cheerio to Sarah. Well, Gerry delayed us *en route* again an' we were held up in Halifax for repairs. Wi' one thing an' another, it was a couple o' months before I was back here in Greenock.

One night when Sarah an' I were sittin' in the kitchen havin' a cup o' tea, I decided to tell her I had been to Kilmarnock. She said, "I know, Tommy."

I looked at her. "You know?" I said. She just nodded an' looked at me wi' an odd expression on her face. "How do you know? Jen wasnae there. There was a nice young girl from downstairs answered the door, but how would she know who I was?"

Sarah said, quiet-like, "That was your own girl, Tom, and she guessed who you were. She said you looked like Hammy."

I was struck dumb. I couldnae say a word. I just got up, put on my coat an' my cap, an' went out an' walked along the bloody seafront till I nearly dropped. Then I went intae a pub an' got fu'.

When the Door Bell Rang

When the doorbell rang, I rushed downstairs expecting to open the door to Ray. Saturday nights we went to the library. Instead of Ray there was a man in uniform. He was looking up and to his right. I saw his straight, unbelted coat, his sharp features and peaked cap silhouetted in the doorway against the grey gloaming light. He looked like Uncle Hammy, but I knew he *couldn't* be Uncle Hammy. He turned to speak to me, and his face merged with the black shadow of cap and coat. I must have heard what he asked, for I answered, "No, she's not at home," and, "I don't know when she'll be back." He was so close. If I had stretched out my hand, I could have touched him. But he left. Even if I had wanted to, I doubt if I could have found the words to hold him there. If I could have said, "Wait! Don't you know who I am?" would he have stayed?

I could have said, "Mum will be home at eight o'clock. She and Jennie are at the pictures. But please come in. I'll make a cup of tea and we can talk. I'll tell you all about myself. You can do the same." But I couldn't.....couldn't speak.

He turned away. I shut the door quickly, shut out night, shadowy form, questioning voice. But the hall was dark and held its own shadows, spectres hovering, lurking still in childhood corners. I had to get away – run – from ghosts – the past – voices – a voice asking more than I could give.

Run! I race through dark, empty streets. Heartbeats, footsteps thunder in my ears. My breath rasps, tears, pains my throat. Cobbles stumble my feet. Hedges grab and claw my hair. A dog yelps, alarmed. Sharp voice raps, "Be quiet!" Be quiet. A door slams. Be quiet, quiet, pounding heart.

At Ray's I lean against the door, shaking legs buckle, arms, hands tingle, bloodless. The leaded glass pane cools my forehead. Glad now of the dark, unseen, I try to breathe without gasping, to soothe my aching throat, still thumping heart. My head is light, as though detached from its body.

Indoors, they ask, do I want tea? I shake my head – I can't ...speak.

I leave with Ray. The familiar streets hold no terror now, my friend beside me. I want to tell her, "My father was here! He came to my house!" but I can't...I can't...speak.

Ray's Story 1998

Hi, you two. God, what a day! I'm fair worn oot. That's what your grandpa would've said. Put the kettle on, Hilary, please, love. I'm dying for a cuppa. The road up to Glasgow was quite good. Not too much traffic. Coming back was a different story. Sal was in plenty of time for her flight, so we had time for a coffee and a last wee blether. God knows when I'll see her again.

You know I told you, Mandy, about the night when Sal and I were kids and her father came to Kilmarnock? I told you too, Hil, didn't I? Yes, I thought so. Well, you'll never believe what I'm going to tell you now. Sal has never really talked about that night, all the years I've known her, but she started on about it at the Dick yesterday when we went to look at the microfiches, and I thought she was a bit mistaken about how some things had happened, so, when we had time before she left this afternoon, I thought I'd just tell her, straighten her out on what really did happen.

You see, *she* thought I'd gone to her house as usual to get her, and then we'd just walked up Dick Road to the library. But that's not how it happened. She landed on our doorstep, white as a sheet, all out of breath, gasping, trembling. Your Gran asked her if she'd like some tea, but she just shook her head. Didn't say a word. Well, I got ready and we left – walked along McKinlay Place, up Glebe Road – Sal was born in Glebe Road, number 41, did you know that? – along Arbuckle Street, into Old Mill Road. When we were passing her house, I said, "Where's your library book? Have you not got a book to return?"

Again she just shook her head, still not saying anything. I was getting worried. We were usually giggling and talking about what boys we might see at the Dick.

We were nearly there when she suddenly stopped, grabbed my arm and said in a funny choked kind of voice, "My father was here."

I said, "What do mean you he was here? Where?" She said he came to their house, asked for her mother and then just left. She didn't say much more than that, except that she didn't tell him her mum was just at the pictures.

I suppose it was looking for her Anderson forebears that prompted her to tell me she had been writing about that night, and the writing seemed to loosen her tongue and let her talk. But when she told me how she had waited at her house for me to call for her, I thought – well, I'd better tell her what really happened. So that's what I did when we were having coffee this afternoon.

You should've seen her face! It was as though a curtain lifted in front of her eyes and she remembered – remembered running through the streets as hard as she could and then standing at our door gasping and gasping to get her breath before she could even ring the door bell. Just imagine! She had blocked that out of her mind all these years. She said, "It was so long before I could say anything, I thought I was never going to speak again."

I said, "Oh, Sal, it wasn't really all that long, honest."

"In a way it was," she said. "Maybe I could speak, but it's taken me years to talk."

Tom's Story

Did ye say ye want tae hear a good story? Well, here's one. When I was fifteen I ran away from home, faked my age and joined the army. A boy in a man's world. Better than a boy in the women's world. Just imagine. A mother and three sisters. Talk about petticoat government!

I liked horses and could ride them, so I enlisted in the cavalry – the Royal Scots Greys. Men and horses. Suited me fine. I became batman and groom to an officer and his horse. Before long my regiment went to Palestine. Then the war came. The horses became jeeps, trucks, armoured cars and tanks. And the boy became a man.

In 1940, based in Haifa, I came back one day from a sortie and one of my mates said, "There was a man here lookin' for you, Tom. Off a ship. But he's away. Had to sail yesterday."

I've often wondered – what would I have done if I'd met my father? Shaken his hand or socked him one? Missed him by a day that time in Haifa. There never was another chance. We moved on – right through the desert campaign: El Alamein, Tobruk, Benghazi, Tripoli. Then Sicily, Italy and France. It was over five years till I got back to Blighty. The first thing I did was look up a girl I'd known at school, and I married her. Aunt Sarah – that's my father's sister – was at the weddin'. She told me later he had really wanted to be there, and she'd had her work cut out convincin' him he wouldnae be welcome.

In September, 1946, I was stationed at Aldershot before bein' posted back to Germany. The news came that he was dead – drowned – at Margate. Fell off the gangway.

Drunk, most likely. I said to my mother I'd go. Nobody else in the family went. Just me. The officials said there was no need for me to identify him; they had done that. How could I have done it anyway? I said, "Well, can I see him?" But they just coughed behind their hands, embarrassed-like, and looked at each other and then at me. One of them said, "He was in the water a long time, son."

I was wearin' my new civvies, and I probably didnae look like somebody that had seen men ploughed into the desert sand by tanks; somebody that had lain, waitin' for daybreak, stretched out in the ruts the treads had dug, alongside the stinkin' corpses. I would like to have seen him – just once. But I suppose they were right. Lookin' at death is probably different when it's your father. At his funeral there were just five of us – three of his shipmates, the padre, and me. They gave me his personal effects. There wasnae much: his other uniform; a few civvies; a wallet and a leather purse for coins, both still dryin' out; a mother-of-pearl handled pen-knife; a white metal watch; some photographs and papers, among them an Order of Service for my weddin'.

IV
DREAMS

Dream Journey

The train, I know, will soon pass the house, cross the bridge over Brougham Street, and gradually shudder to a halt in Prince's Pier Station.

"We're nearly there," I say. I try to keep the excitement from my voice. I look – and look – as we approach the bridge, but there is no house by the railway.

I awake from my dream, one that occurs again and again, to a deep sense of loss, of sadness and regret that the place and the people are no more. The Greenock house, I know, is long gone. In its place, a grassed-over vacant lot, for who, nowadays, would build a house so close to the railway line that one could almost, from a side window, touch the outstretched hand of the engine driver?

Attic Games

I am usually Deanna Durbin in pale green picture hat, ribbons down the back, or in Jennie's mauve taffeta (better not let her catch me!) for my big debut with a hundred men and Mr. Stokowski.

Sometimes I'm Judy Garland in Easter bonnet of dusty-pink straw and bunched unseasonable cherries (Mum's summer hat).

Or I'm Shirley Temple tap-tapping across the lino to the good ship Lollipop, cutely smiling, tossing imaginary curls.

At other times I'm Mickey Rooney, acting tough and cheeky. But he doesn't sing much, so I'm Bobby Breen, crooning Hawaiian songs to sliding steel guitars.

Then I'm the dusky girl he's singing to. Arms ripple, hips wiggle in innocent seduction, my hula skirt an old lace curtain.

But brides wear lace, so I float down the aisle, radiant on my father's arm.

 My diamond tiara and his admiral's gold braid glitter in candlelight.

Wedding of the Year – Hollywood-style.

Dream Ship

From the attic window I peer with my magic telescope and find the little ship. The helmsman, in red bandana and jaunty cap, steers through green, white-crested waves that part for him like railway lines. He smiles and waves; he can see me though I'm far away. His brother has worked his magic in the engine room and now stands profiled in the stern, triple-tonguing on his cornet to the top of the octave. The exuberant sounds leap and rebound among the green and purple hills along the firth – *Carnival of Venice* on the Clyde!

I follow the ship as it heads for port and – with my magic telescope – see, deep in the hold, its cargo: *Cherry Blossom* boot polish, *Cuticura* shaving soap, *Evening in Paris* perfume, playing cards for Sunday games, gramophone records for Saturday dances, cream cookies and pies for homecoming teas, dolls with long-fringed lashes, chocolates in gold boxes for special treats.

It will soon be arriving at Prince's Pier, so I hurry downstairs from the attic – down – down – and out, and across Brougham Street, up the station approach (I'm wearing my navy sailor dress and white sandals) through the sunny glass-roofed station, under the fuchsia baskets hanging purple and pink, right to the pier. I must be there when they dock to wave and shout, "It's me! I'm here! I'm here!"

I Dream about Grey Houses

I dream that we move to a new old house with rooms opening one upon the other. But water cascades from the roof, pours through the ceiling with its crumbling plaster and soaks the beds underneath. I don't know what to do. I don't know how to stop the water. I don't know if the water is coming from rain or from the iron pipes that burst in winter.

Why do we say the pipes burst when they only crack? To burst is to explode. An explosion of metal. Water pours in torrents from pipes as wide as portholes or jagged tears in the grey steel hull. The room shrinks, crowding the men to a shallow space under the ceiling. The white paint flakes above their scrabbling fingers. Their beds levitate around them like magic carpets waiting to fly them on some great adventure.

Her Mother

The ten-year-old girl wears a navy-blue dress with white polka dots, white piqué collar. When the dress is washed, the collar is taken off, washed separately, starched, ironed, stitched on again. Her mother does this: makes all her dresses, coats, skirts, blouses – from remnants – or scraps from clothes she makes for other people.

She loves the fabrics, names them, touches them like children who are dear to her,

     calico   *cambric*   *muslin*

pins the delicate paper to the cloth, cuts and snips, chalks and cuts again.

     tarlatan   *organdy*   *organza*

She has a talent for seeing where the pieces fit, can see the end result.

     sateen   *moygashell*   *sharmoline*

When the pieces are sewn together, she tries the dress on her daughter, kneels, the wooden pin dish (once red, but scratched by the pins to a pale pink) on the floor beside her.

     tweed   *gabardine*   *velour*

She puts pins in her mouth, where her fingers can find them, must keep her eye on the hem as the girl turns, stops, turns again.

viyella   *mohair*   *cashmere*

When she sets in the sleeve and pins the darts around the small waist, she bends over, their faces close.

georgette   *tulle*   *chiffon*

The weave of lines around her eyes is like fine linen. A wisp from the light brown hair could touch her daughter's cheek.

velvet   *gros-grain*   *taffeta*

Her breath is warm and almost sweet as she speaks in the only language she knows.

satin   *crêpe de chine*   *Shantung silk*

Why Art Thou Silent?

Mother sang:

Oh, hast thou forgotten how soon we must sever?
Oh, hast thou forgotten this day we must part?
It may be for years and it may be forever.
Then why art thou silent, thou voice of my heart?
Why art thou silent, Kathleen Mavourneen?

When she spoke, her words were guarded,
purged of most endearments.
A word like *love* was foreign,
from a language she did not speak,
caress an alien action.

She would clutch my hand tightly
to cross dangerous King Street,
or hurry me along busy London Road.

But once, when I was ill,
she took me into the big, cool bed
where she slept alone,
and held my hand for a long time.

We lay content – like lovers.

She did not speak,
but I heard the voice of her heart.

Dream Songs

Dream lullabies for bairnies
echo through my aging nights.

A ghost cornet,
faintly heard in the lonely dawn,
plays an Irish song
lamenting a long-ago love.

We have heard them,
Margaret and I,
with the ear that's tuned
to hear the sounds
that might have been.

Perhaps One Day

In my house dream
I open door after door,
expect to find someone
waiting.

It is always light
in the doorway,
brilliant blue
but empty.

Perhaps one day
when I sleep,
a door will open.

I'll see a figure,
hand outstretched,
and I'll follow it
through the doorway
into the light.

11. *Left*: Self aged 14

12. *Below*: Sisters Margaret aged 12, and Jennie, aged 15

13. *Below*: Friend Ray L. and self, Kilmarnock, 1950

14. Brother Tom, *Royal Scots Greys* recruit, 1938

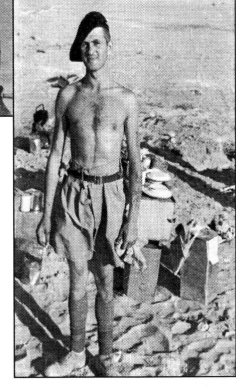

15. Tom, North African Desert Campaign, 1942

V
REFLECTIONS

Departure

We stood on deck on the *Empress of Canada*, a small family, parents and two children, choking back tears as we watched Jennie move down the gangway, along the pier, into the shed and out of sight. At the foot of the gangway, she had turned to wave, a plump middle-aged figure in a summer dress, straight-backed, hair still blonde, the familiar tight-lipped smile meant to conceal her pain.

She had accompanied us to Liverpool, the point of embarkation, and now had to return alone to the home in London she shared with Margaret, where together they would grieve, perhaps forever, the loss of their so much younger sister and her children, for we were the only children they had ever truly known.

How often has this scene been enacted: the grieving relatives on dockside or in airport departure lounge, and the emigrants, taking with them, besides their goods and chattels and plans for a better life, a burden of guilt for the sadness caused to dear ones left behind? Air travel has now made possible visits from relatives and return visits "home", but every parting renews the hurt, until, in time, the separation is forever.

Those of us who have made that one way journey, by whatever means and for whatever reasons, know the hopes and fears of facing the unknown. If we in modern times have felt apprehension for an uncertain future, what must have been the terrors of those who were driven from their homeland by the knout of the czar, the famine of the potato blight, and the butchery and treachery of the Jacobite Rebellion and its aftermath, the suppression of the clans and the Highland Clearances? Whatever their dreams for the future might have been, the hope of seeing again their native land and their loved ones could not have been one of them.

In a prairie city I live on a street intersected by others with Scottish names: Hamilton, McIntyre, Angus, Rae, Cameron, Athol, Argyle and many more. The people for whom these streets are named may have been descendants of those who found refuge in Atlantic Canada or in the settlements of Ontario and Manitoba before moving further west, perhaps by railroad – Sir John A. Macdonald's dream. Or, lured by the government's promise of free land for homesteaders, they may have journeyed the long, dusty miles by Red River cart, to scratch a living from the barren prairie and make peace with those whose land they had usurped. But in July of 1965, those speculations were in the future. When we had waved our goodbyes to Jennie, my husband and I shepherded our bewildered children back to the cabin to help them and each other into life jackets. Boat drill was in half an hour.

Clans of a Different Race

we   came with nothing
will   ask for little but to
go   back in dreams feeling the smirring wind
on   faces turned to the east
until   sea-scent catches the heart and
we   hear in the mind's ear the gulls' wailing lament that we
are   gone
gone   from their island
and   here
on   our homestead island shored by
the   sun-baked fire-guard
prairie   seas of green waved with gold lap
the   sour alkaline beach
ghosts   walk with us
who   knew no shore but their
own   shell-scattered sands
it   seems strange that we
continue   our half-life unused
to   this vast plain
walk   unhidden by heather
in   purple glens while
clans   of a different race are here
searching   like us
for   their lost ways
food   scarce
and   hunger lurking at the tipi flap
for   the unprepared
what   can they do
they   wait like us for spirit chiefs to raise them
once   more with the cry they
knew   long ago

Word/line acrostic from *like a river* by John Newlove

Arrival

In the end, the city appeared quite suddenly before our straining eyes. One moment, there had been only the vast, flat land with the vaster sky above. Next, with but a blink of the eye, it was there, spread out across the horizon, a distant shore on the prairie sea. The monotony and fatigue of the three days' train journey, after five days at sea, disappeared as suddenly as the city had appeared. With growing anticipation we watched the indiscernible outline on the horizon assume the shapes of assorted buildings. The evening sun caught up the beginning glints of gold in the ripening grain, waving and nodding its welcome under the banner sky, blue as the saltire. The train sped – or crept – through the green-gold, sunlit evening, towards our hopes and dreams. Although the journey had been long, it seemed appropriate that we were arriving by train to begin our new life.

My childhood trains had always taken me to places of adventure: day trips to the seaside, outings to the theatre in Glasgow, and, especially, visits to my Greenock relatives. The network of railway lines connecting my home town of Kilmarnock with the Clyde coast towns, and with Glasgow and Greenock, was the sole means of travel for my family in the 1930's.

Now there are motorways with quaintly called dual carriageways, cloverleafs and flyovers that speed cars and buses from inland towns to the coast in minutes. The twenty miles from Kilmarnock to Glasgow can be a jaunt before breakfast, and Greenock, while less accessible, can be easily reached across-country, instead of by train to Glasgow and thence on a different railway line to Greenock. Of course, there are still trains, but they are electrified. The steam locomotives that puffed and shrieked and jabbered, as though in constant argument with themselves or with each other, are long gone. And so is the train that brought us, an immigrant family, to the Saskatchewan prairie. The journey that ended here that summer evening was my last train ride. Now, departing or arriving, we fly over a patchwork of wheatfields; lakes like silver florins scattered from a generous hand; and ribbons of river. An eagle's view under the silent, brilliant blue.

But who can forget the noisy clamour of iron wheels on steel, the stench of soot and chuffing steam, and the sting of sea-laden wind as you lean from the carriage window. You are waiting – waiting – for the train to slow – and slow – and slow – and stop – at last.

Family Picture

They always called their parents Mummy and Daddy – my unmarried, elderly sisters – who lived to remember the past.

In a snapshot I once had, a man reclines on a car rug (it would be a tartan plaid). He leans on one elbow, legs rather stiff and straight, wears a dark suit and tie, flat cloth cap, stares into the camera, serious, but does not seem unhappy.

His wife sits or kneels behind, caught by the camera pinning up her hair (I know it is light brown like the photograph, fine, always loosening). Her right hand is at her mouth, in which she has the hairpins; her left is curved above her, a ballerina's, bent elegantly at the wrist. Fingers touch her crown to secure the straggling wisp. She looks down, a frown of concentration, but does not seem unhappy.

The little boy sits in front of his daddy, solemn, in the manner of small boys told to watch the birdie.

The two girls, one either side of their mummy, are smiling: one mischievous, dark disheveled bob; the other sedate, long straight hair a golden cape around her shoulders.

This was the only picture of our parents with three of their children, the faded sepia proving more than just imagined happiness, but now it is lost.

Over the years, each of us, when turning out the box of

snapshots, souvenirs, family memorabilia, has lingered over it.

My sisters, I think, would relive that family outing: their father on the motorbike, leather coat and goggles; their mother arranging her long skirts to cling behind him; they and their little brother snug and secure in the deep side-car. When I was little I would ask, "But where am I?" They'd laugh, try to explain.

Today, the picture is only in my mind. I am still somewhat little, and now, quite old. But I know I was there in the smile of one, the eyes of another, and the loosening light brown hair.

Wedding Ring

When our mother was cremated, my sister Jennie said,
"We'll leave the ring.
She was the only one it meant anything to."

If we had looked in the ashes,
would we have found a lump of gold,
or a thousand specks among the grey?
Or would it have been there,
a perfect circle still,
refined
by fire?

When our father was buried, Tom asked about the ring.
"We've left it," they said. "We'd have to cut it off.
You want that?"

He said, "No",
knowing what machines can do
to bloated flesh.

In an English seaport town,
sandy earth,
the grey-white bones lie
unmarked.
On one skeletal finger,
un-glinting,
lacking light,
the ring remains
intact.

Eleven Old Mill Road, Kilmarnock

Our house stood, relic of a grander age of horse and carriage,
tea in the drawing room at four.
We played lords and ladies in the parlour.
The ivory-handled levers on the wall beside the mantel
no longer jangled bells in distant kitchens below stairs,
but summoned ghost servants to our games.

We lived there, joint-tenants with strangers: two families –
children, cats, dogs crowded into once elegant rooms –
with prams, toys, coal scuttles,
sewing machines, air-raid wardens' gear.

The *News of the World* reported murder and rape;
Churchill proclaimed our finest hour.

Now, the house is gone;
in its place a block of flats,
grey-white roughcast superimposed
on black dirt mixed with rubble:
shards, splinters of former lives
razed, levelled,
grey sandstone turned to dust.

Forever

My mother and Aunt Sarah were friends. Travelling their respective journeys by train, they would meet for a day's shopping in Glasgow. I often went with them. I remember the winter outings best: the walk from Saint Enoch's Station; morning frost on the cobbles of Argyle Street; the clop and clatter of Clydesdales hauling drays; breath from their steaming and snorting nostrils; the clang of tramcars swinging up into Renfield Street; the sun struggling through lingering fog; and Aunt Sarah smiling her greeting, her cheek cool through the silky veil of her hat.

I suppose on these days when my attention was elsewhere, my mother would get news of my father, but if she did, it was never shared – with my older sisters perhaps, but with me – no. Her determination to keep me from all knowledge of him, other than the barest facts, was something I only sensed, because even that was never expressed, and I must have quickly learned to ask no questions. But if she didn't talk, neither did she condemn, nor even criticize.

Many years later, I learned – from Aunt Sarah – how my mother had tried and tried to help my father. They had even planned a fresh start in Canada or America. But when I was born, she decided to leave him and raise her children on her own. Whether he had been on shore jobs or at sea, money from him was at best sporadic, often non-existent. So, who could blame my mother? With her skills as a dressmaker to earn her an income, she set about re-making our lives. But the thought that without that fourth child – myself – the family might have survived its crises and remained intact has always been with me. The effects of that decision, made so many years ago, remained, indelible, spreading through the fabric of our lives and resisting all attempts to remove. For me, the marks have faded with the years, but I know they will be there, in the fibres, as they were with my sisters and my brother, to the end.

But the marks of love and friendship also endured. My mother and my father's sister were made sisters forever, not only in law but in love, and I was linked to both forever, by the same man, the same absent presence in our lives.

Compensation

In 1944 we were able to buy a house of our own and leave the old grey house with its dingy gas-lit rooms, attic play-room, lean-to coal cellar, and all its war-time memories of air-raid sirens, blacked-out windows and doors, and dark hall-ways. But the memories were re-awakened when one day, about two years later, a telegram arrived, not from the shipping company, but from Aunt Sarah in Greenock. She had been notified of my father's death because her house in Brougham Street was his home. The telegram said he had been drowned at Margate, a little south-east England seaside town as far from the dangers of Atlantic convoys as one could imagine. We later learned that while board-ing his boat, a small merchant vessel that plied the coastal waters around Britain, on a dark night, he had fallen from a badly-lit temporary gangway.

It was my job to write to the Seamen's Union to press our case for compensation. Compensation for what, I wondered. But the shipping company obligingly paid some hundreds of pounds.

My father's death provided my mother with more money than she had had from him in many a long day. With it she bought a set of six walnut spoon-back chairs, which now grace my Canadian home.

The Burns Connection

On my living room wall, close to, and at right angles to the window, hangs a picture of Robert Burns. It is a print taken from an etching of Burns in his Masonic regalia as Depute Master of Lodge Saint James, Tarbolton, a village some eight miles from Kilmarnock. This picture hung on our parlour wall near a sepia-toned, photo portrait of my mother as a young woman. It seems to me entirely logical that, as a small child, I should have one day asked the family in general, "Is that man my daddy?" The question could have been met with laughter, but no one laughed. Instead, my mother, perhaps to avoid any further questions about the person whose identity it was not, gave me my first lesson on the national bard. But it was a long time before I realized that the "common" street language she discouraged me from speaking was, in fact, the dialect in which the revered Burns's best work had been written.

I have never regretted that I learned to speak English with a passable "educated" accent, but neither have I regretted that I absorbed, in a working class background, a language more ancient and more expressive by far than standard English, a language that has united not only Scots the world over, but the world itself with the directive that "auld acquaintance" shouldn't be forgot; that we should "tak a cup o' kindness yet/ for auld lang syne" And today, half a world away from where these words were penned, I find myself reaching back, far back, with the long fingers of memory, to touch again the gold I left behind on my own doorstep.

"Rabbie", as I affectionately call him, looks out from

my high third floor window, across the clusters of buildings in the neighbourhood, to the prairie beyond, and away to the west. And my mother, who sang his songs, still regards him from her place on the window wall, a half smile on her lips, light brown hair a wide bouffant around her face, a locket and lace at her throat.

But the photograph of my mother I cherish most was taken, by me, on my son's christening day in November, 1957, two months before her death. That gentle smile and those soft eyes spoke to me always, when no words could, and they speak to me still.

Riches for a Lifetime

I know I have not said enough
about love

the kind that
       stitched long hours of the night
       with the fine white thread of light
       under the sewing room door

the kind that
       kept the inside pocket of the household purse
       for hard-earned shillings
       twenty-one and there's a guinea
       currency for lessons

       dancing   drama
       singing   piano

       riches for a lifetime

she lacked the words to talk of love
but I can never say enough

Adam

In Saskatchewan, thirty thousand years ago, the relentless ice forced its will on the vast plain stretched before it, and the Qu'Appelle Valley was born. Now, among its rounded green hills, voices call to me. (*Qui appelle?*) Children from the piping school in kilts and T-shirts practise their tunes commemorating ancient battles and heroes long since dead: *Up the Blue Bonnets, Bonnie Dundee, Hieland Laddie*. Then they play *The Green Hills of Tyrol*. Nothing in this tune about wars between Scotland and its English enemies, but something in it stirs the blood. *There was a soldier, a Scottish soldier, who wandered far away and soldiered far* away...Their steps that were lagging under the noon-hot sun have a little more spring. They march on the spot, and their kilts swing a little higher round their boney, sun-tanned knees.

Once when I was visiting Aunt Sarah during the war, Adam was on shore leave and he came up to let us see his new baby. We were in the parlour, and through the open window came the sound of a pipe band far below us on the esplanade playing *The Green Hills of Tyrol*. The baby was crying and Adam, as he had seen women and probably his own father do many times, took the tartan wool rug – the plaid – from the back of the sofa and, wrapping it round both himself and the baby to give it comfort and support, marked time gently to the music. Swaying a little to the rhythm, as though imagining the tartan he wore was swinging high with every step, he quietly hummed till his baby fell asleep.

Seaman's Lullaby

Sh, bairnie, sh!
Dinna greet, ma dearie.
Come tae Dad, ma bonnie lamb,
Ah'll kiss awa' the tearie.

Your Daddy has a great big boat
for sailin' owre the sea.
An' if ye're good an' greet nae mair,
Ah'll tak ye there wi' me.
Sh, bairnie, sh!

16. Father,
Tom Anderson, 1946

17. Mother,
Jen Anderson, 1957

78

Epilogue:

Reconciliation 2005

Today I put your picture on the mantel
beside my mother's; free-standing, curved frames.

You look a little to your left, she looks a little to her right,
eyes almost meet. Hands could touch. Did you speak?

For the first time, grey, slightly wrinkled,
you are together –
as you never were in life.

I know there was a time when eyes met,
hands touched, promises were made.
But that was long ago.

And you, my father, regard me now –
as you never did in life –
with my son's eyes, under brooding, lowered lids.

I know that you would brood alone,
leave the fellowship of other solitary men in seaport bars;
find refuge, solace in the pulsing uterine space
deep within the belly of the ship;
replenish the quickly draining glass,
toast each new-made, teary resolution,
cabin door secure against the world.

Now, I have brooded too,
and know
there was no help for it.

Sally Crooks was born in Kilmarnock, Scotland. She trained in music and theatre arts at the Guildhall School of Music and Drama, London, England, and subsequently, for several years, pursued a career in those areas in Great Britain.

In 1965, with her husband and two children, she immigrated to Regina, Saskatchewan. After obtaining a Bachelor of Education degree from the University of Saskatchewan, Regina Campus, she taught English and pursued her interest in music and related arts, specifically singing, acting and directing, both in schools in which she taught and in the larger community. She has been writing non-fiction and poetry for a number of years with publications in literary magazines and anthologies.

ISBN 141206965-3

9 781412 069656